CBT
ACTIVITIES FOR
KIDS 8-12

Interesting Therapy Exercises to Manage Emotions, Fear, ADHD Issues
and Improve Positive Thinking

By

I. Stallworth

Legal Notice

This book is copyright protected. It is only to be used for personal purposes. Without the author's or publisher's permission, you cannot paraphrase, quote, copy, distribute, sell, or change any part of the information in this book.

Disclaimer Notice

This book is written and published independently. Please keep in mind that the material in this publication is solely for educational and entertaining purposes. All efforts have provided authentic, up-to-date, trustworthy, and comprehensive information. There are no express or implied assurances. The purpose of this book's material is to assist readers in having a better understanding of the subject matter. The activities, information, and exercises are provided solely for self-help information. This book is not intended to replace expert psychologists, legal, financial, or other guidance. If you require counseling, please get in touch with a qualified professional.

By reading this text, the reader accepts that the author will not be held liable for any damages, indirectly or directly, experienced due to the use of the information included herein, particularly, but not limited to, omissions, errors, or inaccuracies. As a reader, you are accountable for your decisions, actions, and consequences.

About the Author

I. Stallworth is a Psychologist with eight years of experience. Throughout her career, she has helped clients with a broad range of issues. She has also collaborated in executive coaching programs in addition to teaching at two different universities.

She is well-versed in conventional therapy practices, having studied them in-depth and putting them into practice for a number of years. She treats her clients with empathy, compassion, and understanding. She has worked with a wide variety of issues related to mental health, such as depression, mood disorders, anxiety and stress management, trauma, and PTSD.

Contents

CHAPTER 6 PARENTS' GUIDE TO TACKLE ANXIETY AND STRESS 64

INTRODUCTION

It's common for children to show feelings of insecurity, worry, and dread from time to time. Anxiety in children usually comes in waves and does not last long.

As children get older, they become concerned about a variety of issues. They may be concerned about getting sick or wounded while they are young. The concentration gets less definite as children grow older and into adolescence. For example, people may spend much time thinking about war, natural, economic, and political concerns, and family connections.

It can also have an impact on their physical well-being. They may feel anxious, shaky, or breathless. They may have stomach butterflies, a hot cheek, clammy palms, a parched tongue, or a rapid heartbeat.

The "fight or flight" reaction is responsible for these anxiety symptoms. This is the body's natural reaction to a threat. It causes the body's natural substances to be released. These chemicals prepare us to face a serious threat. Heart rate, respiration, muscles, nerves, and digestion are all affected. This reaction is designed to keep us safe from harm. The "fight or flight" reaction is hyperactive in mental disorders. Even when there is no real threat, it happens.

The most common treatment for mental disorders is cognitive-behavioral therapy (CBT). This talk therapy teaches families, children, and teenagers how to tackle feelings of dread, anxiety, and concern.

CBT teaches kids that their thoughts and acts have an effect on their emotions and that suppressing their fears just makes them worse. They realize that when they face their fears, they wane and eventually go away.

CBT teaches parents how to respond appropriately when their child is worried. They learn how to assist children in confronting their concerns. Children gain coping strategies to tackle fear and concern more effectively.

The therapist helps the kids to practice this therapy and encourages them through praise and positive feedback. When children address their fears, they might begin to feel better about themselves. They end up getting used to the very things that make them afraid. Having fewer matters to worry enables them to discuss things like school, hobbies, and extracurricular activities. Medicines are sometimes also used to manage symptoms.

Managing symptoms of depression or anxiety can benefit from taking the appropriate medicine and adopting a healthy lifestyle, both. Many things could be at play for youngsters while experiencing anxiety or despair. However, trauma, stress, mistreatment, bullying, abandonment, parental stress or sadness can make some kids more susceptible to anxiety or depression.

Although these characteristics appear to raise the risk of anxiety or depression in youngsters, there are techniques to reduce the likelihood of developing. **CBT Workbook for Kids** is a complete guide to teaching kids to regulate anxiety by using simple, easy, and fun CBT exercises, activities, and games. So why wait? Start reading this book and help your kid with his emotions before it is too late for you to manage.

HI KIDS!

Ferry is an eight-year-old second-grader. Ferry always has been a shy child, as per her mother. Her scores have declined this year, although she generally did well in class. She's also grown unpleasant and introverted. Ferry would only stay with her two best mates at school, whom she has known since kindergarten. She says she is too uncomfortable to socialize with female classmates at lunch and free time.

Ferry became afraid after one of the popular ladies made fun of her for wearing the "dirty" jeans. As a result of her hesitation to dress in front of other females and her fear of embarrassing herself in front of the class, Ferry also skips gym class. She has skipped two birthday sleepovers due to a tummy ache and refuses to participate in any after-school events or groups. Ferry's best friends become irritated since she refuses to do anything with anyone outside of school. Ferry claims that she prefers to spend her time with her younger sister.

Lastly, Ferry's mother has noted that when she's among other kids or people she doesn't know, she has problems with direct eye contact and prefers to mutter and speak quietly. It's been going on for about a year but has worsened in the last six months.

Remember that, separating or isolating yourself from others is not the solution. Work hard, overcome your fears and be a brave person. Otherwise, your friendships and relationships will be in danger like Ferry, and no one would like to talk to you.

CHAPTER 1 CBT: AN EFFECTIVE FORM OF THERAPY

One of the most important lessons we can teach kids is the importance of understanding how ideas may affect their emotions and actions. Reframing unhelpful thinking and the ideas is essential to negotiating the emotional and personal obstacles faced during childhood when intellectual, interpersonal, and social growth are all at a rapid pace.

Children can benefit from cognitive-behavioral therapy by learning to critically examine and adjust their own patterns of thinking, feeling, and reacting in response to challenging situations. During this critical growth period, knowing that behaviors and emotions can be controlled and managed is important. Self-control, coping skills, emotion control, and emotional awareness can all be improved.

People of all ages, even young toddlers and teenagers, can benefit from talk therapy, such as cognitive behavioral therapy (CBT). The core idea of CBT is how thoughts and feelings affect actions. Even if your child doesn't have a diagnosed mental disorder, CBT can still benefit them.

A predetermined objective and number of sessions both are typical in therapy. With the guidance of the therapist, your child will be able to replace negative thinking patterns with more constructive ones. By using role-playing and other approaches, your child can practice different ways to deal with stressful circumstances.

This chapter discusses the evidence and efficiency of cognitive-behavioral therapy with children, the issues that can be helped by CBT with children and adolescents, and the benefits of using CBT for them.

1.1 CBT and Types

Cognitive behavioral therapy (CBT) is a form of talk therapy developed to aid patients in recognizing negative patterns of thought and behavior and developing new, healthier ones. Therapy puts an emphasis on the here and now, rather than lingering on the past. CBT doesn't "cure" ADHD, but it can help with some symptoms and assist other therapies.

CBT has practical, day-to-day applications for kids. With the help of this therapy, your child will be able to recognize destructive thought patterns and replace them with more positive ones. By gaining new viewpoints, a young person can learn to handle difficult situations more effectively. Several distinct forms of CBT include:

Parent-Child CBT

Children and adolescents with anxiety disorders can benefit from cognitive behavioral therapy, especially when their parents are actively involved in their treatment. CBT is especially helpful since it teaches parents how to care for anxious kids using techniques including psychosocial interventions, individual counseling, caregiver coping, and parental involvement. With the help of their children, the parents participate in this therapy and are essentially taught how to handle their anxieties at home.

Motivational Enhancement Therapy combined with CBT (MET)

Teenagers who receive motivational enhancement treatment (MET), an evidence-based therapy, are intrinsically motivated to alter their behavior. It successfully modifies an adolescent's behavior toward drug and alcohol misuse when MET is combined with group-based CBT. This therapy uses dialogue, coping mechanisms, and motivational interviewing techniques to help develop a strategy to alter his behavior and inspire the young person to follow through. During sessions, the therapist will guide the adolescent to stop using drugs through a structured method and will encourage them on as they make progress. The adolescent would participate in group-based CBT after MET therapy sessions for the best outcomes.

Trauma-Specific CBT

Trauma-focused cognitive behavior therapy was structured to treat kids and teens who have experienced trauma. It helps a lot for treating post-traumatic stress disorder (PTSD), but it also helps with other trauma-related disorders. Similar to cognitive behavioral therapy, it is delivered in front of the child and parents for a limited time (usually six to twenty sessions). Several difficulties related to the child's traumatic experiences are addressed in a trauma-focused CBT session, including behavioral and cognitive impairments, sadness, and anxiety. In order to support and manage the challenges of the child, it helps to build parenting abilities and parent-child interactions.

Individual CBT

In individual cognitive behavioral therapy, one therapist teaches the kid or teenager the skills necessary to overcome his or her issues. This type of therapy is completely focused on the child or adolescent. This variation of CBT successfully treats adolescent substance misuse and childhood depression and anxiety disorders.

CBT and Medicine

Research has indicated that treating a child's or adolescent's anxiety symptoms or depression with cognitive behavioral therapy and psychotropic drugs can be successful. If a member of a child's care team determines that medicine is required for your child's therapy, they will be able to prescribe the appropriate dosage.

Group CBT

Along with the kid or adolescent and the therapist, group cognitive behavioral therapy typically involves new acquaintances who are being treated for the same disorder and people from outside the child or adolescent's social circles. Participants in group therapy often share commonalities in their struggles to control their behavior. In addition to learning how to modify one's behavior, participants in group CBT also have the opportunity to form supportive relationships. Group CBT is frequently less expensive and more widely accessible as compared to individual CBT. It is successful in treating adolescent depression and substance dependence.

1.2 Issues that CBT can Address

CBT might give your youngster practical tips for enhancing their current situation. They can carry these new talents with them throughout life as they develop into habits.

Children who use CBT can gain control:

√ Negativity in one's thoughts

√ Impulsivity

√ Defiance

√ Tantrums

Negative responses are replaced with:

√ Better sense of self

√ New coping strategies

√ Aptitude for solving issues

√ More restraint

CBT can assist you irrespective of the kind of mental health problem your kid has. However, it has proven to be an effective method of treating some specific conditions, including:

Substances Abuse

Age range of 12 to 17 years is critical for teens. In order to deal with the emotional and social stresses that might arise during the transition from childhood to adulthood, many young people use drugs.

According to research, CBT is useful in treating teenage substance abuse. However, combining CBT with motivational enhancement therapy is as successful and guarantees that young clients are committed to treatment and motivated to improve their behavior before CBT even starts.

Autism Spectrum Disorder and Anxiety

Teens with high-functioning autism spectrum disorder frequently struggle with anxiety. A CBT program was developed for preteens with autism spectrum disorders and clinical anxiety in a 2015 study. The plan emphasized:

√ Exposure

√ Putting illogical beliefs to the test

√ Behavioral assistance

√ Key components of treatment for autism spectrum disorder

Only 33 kids between 11 and 15 were enrolled in the little study. Parents claimed that CBT reduced the severity of anxiety symptoms.

Bullying

Bullying is a common occurrence among kids and teenagers. Children who experience bullying are more likely to experience sleep issues, self-harm, anxiety, and depression. A disparity, aggressive conduct, and repeated acts of "harm doing" are all hallmarks of bullying.

For adolescent boys experiencing bullying at school, the efficacy of CBT therapy investigated through a research found to massively reduce bullying-related ego anxiety and despair, and its positive effects persisted three months following the intervention.

ADHD

Children with ADHD could have trouble staying still and might act impulsively. Although there are medications to treat this illness, they aren't always the best or only option. Some youngsters still experience persistent symptoms despite taking medicine. According to research, CBT may be more effective than medication alone for some adolescents.

Injuries and PTSD

CBT has been demonstrated as an effective short- and long-term therapy for children and teenagers with post-traumatic stress disorder (PTSD). A 2011 assessment discovered appreciable progress at the 18-month and 4-year follow-ups. Even for young children, CBT is beneficial for treating acute and persistent PTSD following various traumatic experiences. Additionally, CBT may be useful in treating:

√ Teen substance abuse

√ Bipolar illness

√ Depression

√ Erratic eating

√ Obesity

√ An obsessional condition (OCD)

√ Self-harm

With the support of more realistic thought patterns and adaptive coping mechanisms, cognitive-behavioral therapy confronts unhelpful habits and maladaptive thoughts. These alterations may aid in changing the signs and symptoms of various childhood and adolescent-related problems.

Bedwetting

Nocturnal enuresis, the medical term for bedwetting, has been linked to emotional and behavioral issues and may contribute to low self-esteem.

While bedwetting is more common in younger children, it is believed that 3% of youngsters between the ages of 12 and 15 are bed-wetters.

According to research, children and adolescents who underwent cognitive behavior therapy had a higher likelihood of remaining dry for three weeks than those who did not. Additionally, compared to participants utilizing an enuresis alarm, a typical treatment for bedwetting, those undergoing CBT had a lower relapse rate. The symptoms of bedwetting, such as poor self-esteem, anxiety, and shame, can also be helped by CBT.

Mood and Anxiety Disorders

Children and teenagers with anxiety and mood disorders have been demonstrated to respond well to CBT. The effectiveness of CBT as a first-line treatment for children with anxiety disorders has received "strong support."

Parents might also play a part. CBT with active parental involvement showed promise as a successful therapy for children with anxiety ages 3 to 10.

A Low Sense of Self

Low self-esteem has been related to a number of mental illnesses, including melancholy, obsessive-compulsive disorder, binge eating, self-harm, and substance abuse.

In depressed teenagers between the ages of 13 and 18, adolescents who receive CBT appear to have higher self-esteem than those who receive interpersonal therapy.

Intentional Self-Harm

Early adolescence is when recurrent deliberate self-harm (DSH), which has a high association with suicide, typically starts. According to estimates, the average lifetime prevalence of DSH ranges from 7.5% to 8% for preadolescents to 12% to 23% for adolescents.

DSH actions can range from intentional self-poisoning and cutting to repetitive head-banging, which is more frequently seen in young children. A skill-focused modified form of therapy called cognitive behavior therapy (CBT) has shown promising results for the treatment of DSH. After 8–12 individual CBT sessions, DSH behavior in adolescents considerably improved.

Disorder of the Oppositional Defiant

One of the most common causes for referrals to pediatric outpatient mental health services is disruptive conduct, such as angry or aggressive outbursts. A persistent pattern of antagonistic, aggressive, and angry conduct toward authority persons is known as oppositional defiant disorder (ODD).

Physical assault, damage, resistance, bitterness, and antagonistic behavior toward classmates, parents, educators, and other expert figures are just a few behavioral conducts children with ODD may display.

Through CBT, a kid can understand how to deal with issues and speak in a regulated manner, which has significantly reduced ODD. Children's treatment shows greater success when they are accompanied by a trusted adult.

Eating Disorders

Eating disorders are significant psychological problems that are very common and frequently manifest throughout puberty. Girls aged 6 to 12 exhibited weight-related worries at a rate of 40 to 60 percent, and by the age of 20, 13% had eating disorders.

Studies on adolescent boys with eating disorders indicate an increase in the prevalence of these conditions, with boys most frequently diagnosed with an eating issues at age 13.

Eating disorder patients who undergo cognitive-behavioral therapy see improvements in their negative body- and self-image-related thoughts and behaviors. Adolescents who had previously binged showed binge-free behavior after receiving group CBT therapy. Additionally, a 60-week follow-up showed that CBT treatment tailored for teenagers significantly improved weight gain, weight maintenance, and eating disorders.

1.3 Benefits of Using CBT for Kids

Typically, a treatment plan is developed after goals are discussed by the kid, the parent or caregiver, and the therapist. In CBT, problems are solved in a structured manner over several sessions. Depending on the individual and goals, it could take six to twenty sessions.

CBT is a form of talk therapy that goes beyond talking. The therapist will work with you to give your child concrete tools to help them feel more in control and independent. This knowledge will be immediately applicable.

CBT can be given to your child alone or with any other therapy they may require, including prescribed drugs. The treatment strategy can be modified to account for regional or cultural variations.

Research Based Benefits

√ People who are sad have unique thoughts and beliefs that contribute to their melancholy disposition and behaviors. People who are depressed frequently only recall the unfortunate events of their past and concentrate on them, ignoring the good ones. Between 35 and 40% of teenagers experience a severe depressive episode at some moment, with genetic susceptibility to depression and exposure to psychosocial stresses such parental divorce, mortality, and abuse serving as the two main risk factors.

√ Evidence-based CBT has been demonstrated to be effective for a variety of issues. Sixty percent or more of kids and teens with anxiety problems see considerable improvement after receiving CBT, according to meta-analyses. Four years following treatment, according to studies of children who got therapy in community mental health clinics, such recovery rates are definitely still there. Studies show that after getting CBT, the severity of many ADHD-afflicted teenagers' symptoms decreases noticeably. Individualized trauma-focused CBT can significantly reduce PTSD, depressive, and anxiety symptoms in children with PTSD. In one study, after undergoing CBT, 92% of participants no longer encountered the norms for PTSD. After a six-month follow-up, this improvement was still present.

√ Cognitive behavioral therapy is based on the behavioral and psychological theories of human psychopathology. CBT has been found to be an effective treatment for a wide range of psychiatric problems in adults by targeting multiple areas of vulnerability simultaneously using developmentally guided techniques and varying intervention routes.

√ Children and teenagers' most common psychopathology is anxiety disorder. Children often dwell on their own health, the health of those they care about, their schooling, how other people see them, and social issues.

√ Due to their inexperience with coping mechanisms and fear about potential negative outcomes, young people may experience a variety of negative effects. Evidences from clinical trials show that CBT is useful in helping kids who are dealing with anxiety. After treatment, 55–65% of kids no longer reported anxiety. Children as young as seven years old may find CBT helpful for managing mild to moderate anxiety.

√ Positive emotions and healthy relationships can be fostered through CBT's use of behavioral strategies aimed at recognizing and replacing negative beliefs.

√ In adolescents and young adults (ages 11-16) with autism, group cognitive behavioral therapy has been demonstrated to improve creativity and social skills with decreasing self-reported social isolation and stress.

√ After one year of treatment, the prevalence of depressive disorder was reduced in teenagers who participated in a group CBT program that included depression counseling with CBT. It was hypothesized that children and teens who report having severe depressive symptoms would benefit from school-based CBT prevention.

√ Treatment with cognitive-behavioral techniques enhances social skills, self-control, emotions of self-efficacy, analytical problem-solving ability, and participation in rewarding or empowering activities. Children between the ages of 7 and 15 who receive CBT therapy may report less anxiety, better coping skills, and enhanced emotional awareness and control.

√ Children who use CBT can learn how to understand and control their emotions. When they can accomplish this well, kids and teenagers have a 60% decreased risk of acquiring mental problems in later life.

√ When applied to children with ADHD, multicomponent CBT has the potential to bring about re-education, redefinition, and remediation. The most effective CBT groups for ADHD children and teens are those with stress collaboration, anger management techniques, focusing defining and achieving goals, and guidance in developing social skills

√ With the use of CBT, children who are unable or unwilling to speak can nevertheless express their emotions in a variety of ways. An examination of CBT program offered in schools found progresses in flexibility, upbeat thinking, logic of control, and a decrease in negative self-talk and poor self-handling strategies.

√ CBT may be helpful for kids and teenagers who display moderate to severe physical aggression, impatience, and anger. Children who undergo CBT learn how to manage their anger and can practice assertive behaviors that can be used in dispute instead of being violent. They can also improve their social problem-solving skills.

√ Children older than seven who get trauma-focused therapy PTSD symptoms, despair, humiliation, and hazardous sexual behaviors related to abuse were all considerably reduced by CBT. When a parent or caregiver participated in CBT, traumatized children experienced considerably higher increases in interpersonal trust and perceived credibility.

√ Since CBT is adaptable, it may suit the needs of patients of varying ages and developmental stages, allowing for more targeted treatment of mental health issues.

√ Biology, stress, and growing academic and social pressures are only some of the potential influences on children and adolescents' sleep habits. Studies have demonstrated that cognitive behavioral therapy can considerably improve sleep duration and sleep quality.

√ During a 12-week program, CBT is reported to be equally as effective at treating OCD in children and teenagers as it is at lessening signs, and a 9-month follow-up revealed significantly lasting improvement.

√ Decreases in headache frequency and migraine-related disability were greater when CBT was used with medication to treat children with chronic migraines.

√ Selective mutism, anxiety disorders, behavioral problems, sexual assault, sleep concerns, acting out behavior, and the consequences of parental divorce on young children can all be treated with cognitive-behavioral play therapy (CBPT). Children acquire new coping mechanisms for trauma during CBPT by acting out scenes that demonstrate healthy ways to deal with painful feelings using age-appropriate props.

√ In a brief study on "school refusal," 88% of individuals who received CBT for anxiety-related school rejection reported better attendance.76% of participants had normal school attendance after five years and didn't need therapy for school refusal.

1.4 CBT Techniques

Following are some CBT techniques for treatment.

Game Therapy. Using artworks, dolls and toys, or role-playing, the child can discuss problems and think of solutions.

CBT with a trauma emphasis. This method is used to treat kids who have been in traumatic situations like natural disasters. The therapist will focus on the cognitive and behavioral issues brought on by the trauma experienced by the youngster.

Modeling. The therapist may model the desired behavior for the child by acting it out in front of them, for example, by modeling how to handle a bully.

Restructuring. In this way, a youngster can learn to replace negative thoughts with more constructive ones. For instance, "I'm terrible at soccer. I'm not the best soccer player, but I'm good at many other things"; "I'm a complete loser" can be exchanged for it.

Exposure. The child is exposed to things that trigger anxiety in a progressive manner.

Irrespective of the method, CBT can be carried out in several ways.

CHAPTER 2 THE COGNITIVE TRIANGLE

The majority of kids think that emotions just happen to them. They fluctuate, occasionally for no apparent reason, and are challenging or hard to manage. How often have you heard someone describe something as having "made them furious" or "made them anxious"? Even many people feel this way about their emotions. Many people feel somewhat helpless when confronted with powerful emotions like fear and rage.

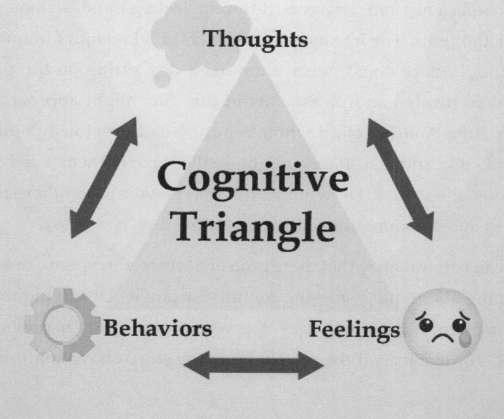

Though it's not quite accurate to say that our emotions are spontaneous, we think about everything that occurs to us throughout the day. Our thoughts guide us how we should feel about what is happening. This method usually works rather well and allows us to make sensible decisions about various scenarios. However, excessively pessimistic beliefs can make anxious children nervous when they don't need to.

The cognitive triangle is a diagram that illustrates the relationships among our thoughts, feelings, and acts. Our thoughts determine how we feel, our feelings determine how we behave, and finally, our actions significantly impact how we perceive the world and potential future thoughts. Teaching a child about the cognitive triangle is a fantastic first step when introducing a child to CBT.

The cognitive triangle can demonstrate how various individuals can share the same experience but arrive at different feelings and actions resulting from their thoughts. For instance, a young child who enjoys animals might think, "Cute, I adore dogs!" when they see a dog sitting on the pavement. She would be thrilled and pleased about this. She might approach the dog and stroke him. Another child whom a puppy had previously bitten might see the same dog and fear that he might do the same to them. He'd be scared and nervous about that. He would probably move to the other side of the roadway to avoid coming into contact with the dog.

Children can better realize that there is no one "correct" response to a situation after learning about and using the cognitive triangle. Observing the vicious cycles that might occasionally develop when a person is nervous can also be helpful. For instance, if the youngster in the story above continues to run away from every dog he encounters, he will never have the opportunity to discover all the amiable dogs that exist in the world. He might always have a fear of dogs.

2.1 Automatic Thoughts vs. Core Beliefs

After teaching a youngster about the cognitive triangle, you can go to the following stage. Because our ideas, feelings, and behaviors are intertwined, altering one of them affects the others. Simply advising someone to quit being anxious is probably not going to have any effect because it's pretty difficult to modify a mood. It's simpler to handle anxiety by altering our thoughts or behaviors.

Your child can modify her thoughts by learning to recognize fears and transform them into something more useful. She can alter her behavior by developing coping mechanisms that help her unwind physically and divert her attention from her problems. In either case, she will be assisting herself in reducing her anxiety or making it a more beneficial emotion to experience.

2.2 What are you Feeling?

I frequently compare kids to "remote controls" when discussing coping and relaxation techniques with them. One method we can alter our behavior to boost our mood is through practices like deep breathing, muscle relaxation, and guided visualization. It can assist children in understanding the purpose behind our repeated instructions to "take deep breaths."

Sometimes focusing on an overwhelming feeling only makes it worse while we're experiencing one. Children who experience worry are prone to ruminating, which is the act of repeating and amplifying fears. Coping mechanisms function like a remote control that enables children to "change the channel" of their emotions by putting them in another. Strong emotion can also be "turned down" so that it is more controllable by using these techniques.

These concepts might be useful when attempting to comfort your worried youngster because most kids are familiar with remote controls and how they operate. Music, physical activity, and guided visualization can all help to change the channel, while relaxation techniques like deep breathing and muscle relaxation can help to lower the volume.

2.3 Behavior Activation

A particular CBT technique is called behavioral activation (BA). In addition to other cognitive behavioral therapy methods, such as cognitive restructuring, it can also be utilized as a stand-alone treatment. Behavioral activation, like cognitive work, helps us to understand how actions affect feelings. Here are some examples of applications for BA:

Jim struggles with anxiety and sadness. He struggles to grasp the reasons behind his mood swings and his temporary improvements in mood. He started to identify previously unnoticed mood triggers as they related to his routine in therapy. He could alter his strategy and become more conscious of these triggers, which finally allowed him to alter his mood.

Debbie was aware that her family background, the strain of caring for her kid with special needs, and the changing of the seasons all contributed to her depression. Despite being aware of the triggers, she has trouble controlling her mood since she frequently lacks the motivation to engage in activities that might alleviate her despair. She frequently convinces herself that she won't exercise until it's warmer outdoors and doesn't feel like calling her friends, who typically make her feel better. Together with her therapist, she started developing techniques for boosting her motivation. These included practicing awareness of various avoidance habits and creating alternate, adaptive actions.

The theory behind behavioral activation is that depression frequently prevents us from engaging in the activities that give our lives delight and significance. This "downward spiral" makes us feel even worse. We use our behaviors and decisions in behavioral activation to break this loop.

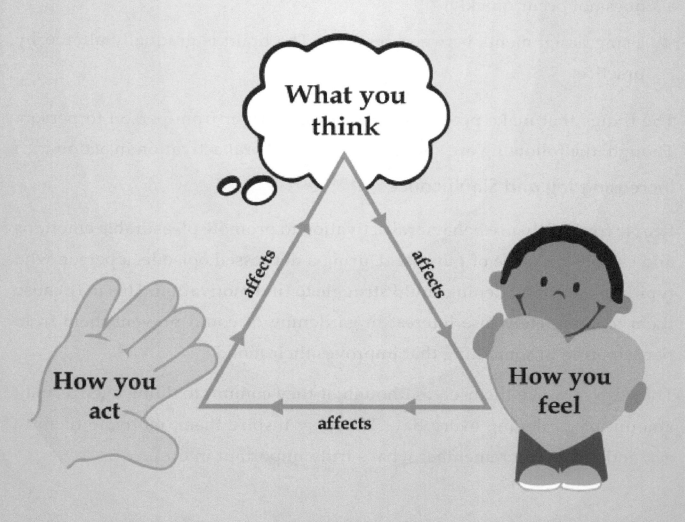

Understanding the "vicious cycles" of depression is one of the behavioral activation activities that is;

√ Keeping an eye on our regular activities

√ Determining objectives and values

√ Increasing motivation and energy.

√ Activity scheduling

√ Addressing issues with potential activation barriers

√ Decrease avoidance

√ Working together to achieve steady, methodical development. Change does not occur quickly!

√ Using assignments between sessions. The brain is gradually altered by practice.

The things that make people feel worthy can differ from person to person. Though, the following are some cases of behavioral activation in action.

Increasing Joy and Significance

People frequently use behavioral activation to promote pleasurable emotions and establish a sense of purpose. During a depressed episode, a person who typically enjoys gardening could struggle to find motivation. This may cause them to completely lose interest in gardening or could prevent them from participating in something that improves their mood.

They can improve themselves, though, if they commit to doing even a small amount of gardening every day. This may inspire them, motivate them to act, and help them remember what's truly important in life.

Changing Harmful Behaviors

Another application of behavioral activation is to replace an unhealthy behavior with a more positive one. When people learn that their usual coping mechanism—drinking alcohol—actually makes them feel worse, they may decide to replace it with something more positive and relaxing, like a creative hobby.

When they do this, they experience positive feelings making it easier for them to refrain from smoking the next time they feel stressed. It also helps with improved stress management without having the harmful impacts of alcohol.

Enhancing Connections

Reaching out to loved ones or participating in group activities may be more challenging when uncomfortable emotions are felt. People might then retreat or isolate themselves as a result of this. This could deepen depression, increase the feelings of isolation, or reduce social support.

To elude this, a person having distress making friends may consider committing to a weekly movie night, regular catch up with a friend, or quality time with their parents. Even if they don't feel like it, participating in these activities could end up making them feel more connected, comfortable, or fun-loving.

Thoughts, Feelings, Actions Worksheet

Link your thoughts with your feelings and actions by imagining any real life situation. Use the worksheet below.

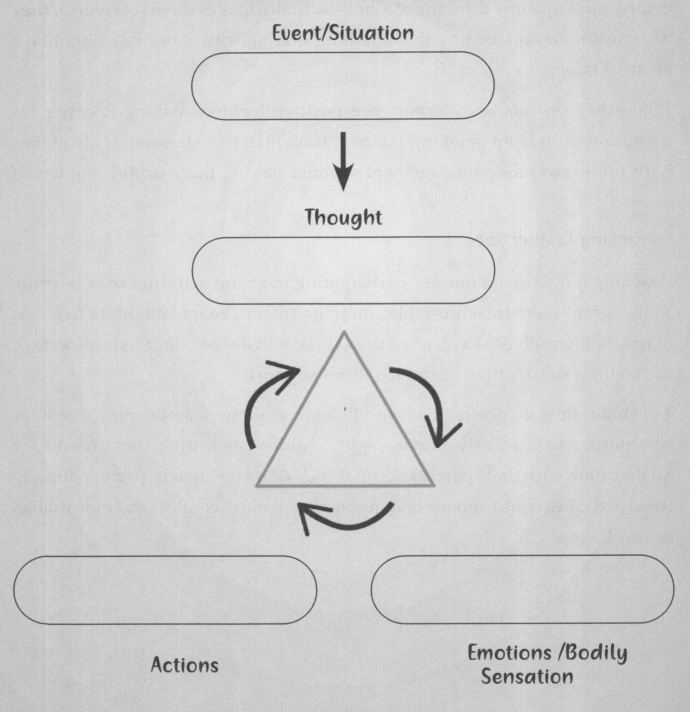

Event/Situation

Thought

Actions

Emotions /Bodily Sensation

CHAPTER 3 TALKING BACK TO WORRIES

Children who receive CBT are taught a "cognitive restructuring" technique to alter their thoughts. I usually refer to it as "talking back" to thoughts because this is the least kid-friendly term imaginable. Before using this strategy, kids must develop the ability to recognize when they are worrying. The next step is to determine whether or not their anxiety is realistic—it typically isn't! Finally, they come up with an alternative that is more constructive and practical that they can use.

You can explain to your child that she won't necessarily learn in CBT to believe in all her anxieties. Her time in therapy will teach her how to recognize her fears and determine whether or not to give them any attention. She will learn how to "speak back" to unhelpful people so that they will stop dictating how she behaves. Use these activities and exercises to talk back to your worries.

3.1 Worry Management

Worry Jar

Write down all the worries in this worry jar.

Worry Says What?

Can you talk back to your following worries?

When worry says, "I can't get good grades." I SAY:

When worry says, "Everyone will laugh at my answer." I SAY:

When worry says, "I'll never be good at this." I SAY:

Draw a picture of your worry monster!

Worrying

Now tell me little bit about your worries.

Worrying Worksheet

I'm worried about _____

Can I do something about it?

Yes: I can _____

No: Then why should I worry?

CHALLENGE
ACCEPTED

I'm worried about _____

Can I do something about it?

Yes: I can _____

No: Then why should I worry?

CHALLENGE
ACCEPTED

I'm worried about _____

Can I do something about it?

Yes: I can _____

No: Then why should I worry?

CHALLENGE
ACCEPTED

Worry Tracker

Track your worries with worry tracker.

My Worry	
Time & Place	
What Happened Before My Worry Started?	
How my Body Felt?	
Strategy I used to Feel Better	

3.2 Fear Management

My Fears

Overcome your fears with this fear sheet.

What are the things that make you nervous?

1.

2.

3.

4.

What does your brain think about when it is scared?

1.

2.

3.

4.

Where do you feel it in your body? Colour in where you can feel it.

1.

2.

3.

4.

What are 3 things that make you feel better?

1.

2.

3.

Fear Worksheet

Tell me about your fears so that I can help you with those.

My biggest fear is

```
[                                                    ]
```

You are usually afraid when

```
[                                                    ]
```

What triggers your fears

```
[                                                    ]
```

Any Physical symptoms that you experience in your body

```
[                                                    ]
```

Any particular event/incident that strengthens your fear

```
[                                                    ]
```

How do you cope with

```
[                                                    ]
```

Climbing My Fear Ladder

It is a ladder for you so that you can gradually climb on it by overcoming your fears. Write your fears and rate them out of 10. Don't forget to write your goal.

What is my goal?

	/10
	/10
	/10
	/10
	/10
	/10
	/10
	/10
	/10
	/10

CHAPTER 4 CBT: A NEW WAY TO PREVENT ANXIETY

"Feeling worried or afraid is part of the human experience. Anxiety and uneasiness are founded in survival. Everyone occasionally feels anxiety to varying degrees. Extreme anxiety, terror, or panic are frequently triggered by thoughts about a situation rather than the circumstance itself.

You can have the strength to tackle a problem if you can put some distance between it and your ideas, feelings, and behavior. It doesn't prevent you from achieving your objective or make things worse. A large portion of our experience is based on perception. The ability to let go of negative thoughts frees us to think about more sensible, factual alternatives, which results in a better experience and less strong unpleasant feelings.

Over time, it can alter your behavior toward a scenario if you have unfavorable feelings and ideas about it. If a child consistently feels bad about attending school, they might start making up reasons not to attend.

These actions begin to repeat themselves over time, forming patterns. It is possible to alter both the patterns themselves and the feelings they evoke through cognitive behavioral therapy. Time may prevent these actions.

Cognitive behavioral therapy (CBT) educates patients on the connectedness of their thoughts, emotions, behaviors, and physical experiences, all of which contribute to the progression of their anxiety and depression. The important thing is that you can intervene to break the cycle of avoiding anxiety-inducing circumstances.

4.1 Anxiety Prevention (For Kids)

Let's take the situation of having poor self-esteem as an example. Perhaps you attempt to avoid social events because being in a crowd makes you feel anxious and overwhelmed. You've been asked to a group meeting at school where you anticipate a sizable turnout. Your first impression is, "No way. I'll have to start a conversation. What if they perceive me as awkward?"

You might experience anxiety or even a little panic. You abruptly inform the teacher that you're feeling under the weather. You can't make it. While engaging in this behavior will temporarily improve your mood, it will worsen your nervousness in social situations. The issue is that consistently avoiding circumstances that make you anxious or afraid perpetuates this unfavorable cycle of thoughts, feelings, and actions.

You address your social anxiety in counseling. You could:

√ Start learning relaxation techniques so you'll be prepared the next time you get a social invitation.

√ When you feel anxious, write down the thoughts that come to mind.

√ Examine your list with your therapist.

√ Replace unfavorable emotions and thoughts with more sensible ones.

√ Reframing is another name for this method of cognitive restructuring.

You will be abler to continue acting in opposition to the dread as you feel yourself becoming adept at handling the things that previously brought to worry and anxiety. CBT practitioners use some standard methods to assist you in controlling your anxiety and altering your behavior.

Restructuring or Reframing of the Mind

Examining unfavorable thought patterns is a necessary step in this process. Maybe you usually:

√ Overgeneralize

√ Pretend the worst will occur

√ Give excessive weight to minute details

This manner of thinking could influence your actions and, in some cases, might become a self-fulfilling prophecy.

Difficulty in Thinking

It's important to think critically and to support your conclusions with data from your own experience. Instead of just thinking that your thoughts are the facts or the truth, thought questioning might help you view things more objectively.

A person who is knowledgeable about cognitive distortions will be able to recognize them when they occur in their thoughts and attempt to replace them with more accurate and balanced ones.

You could find it difficult to reason through your issues while anxious. You could experience anxiety without being aware of where it is coming from. Alternatively, you could fear something like social events but not understand why.

The Stimulation of Behavior

You can schedule an activity if worry prevents you from doing it by noting it on your calendar. Doing this lets you put a plan in place and stop worrying about it.

For instance, if you're concerned that your little sister might get sick at a playground, the CBT tactics will motivate you to act and handle the circumstance.

Journaling

Keeping a thought recorder can help you connect with and become aware of your thoughts and feelings. Additionally, it can aid with cognitive structure and clarity.

List the negative and inspiring ideas you can use in their stead. Your therapist might advise you to journal your new skills and routines outside therapy sessions.

Behavioral Research

When you have catastrophic thinking or expect the worse, you commonly use behavioral research. We create predictions about the potential outcomes of the activity and record what we anticipate and what we fear. It can be a good idea to discuss your predictions and whether they came true with your therapist. The likelihood of your worst-case scenario happening will soon dawn on you.

Calming Techniques

Relaxation techniques reduce stress and enhance clear thinking. These, in turn, might help you regain control of a situation. These techniques can include the following:

√ Engaging in deep breathing exercises

√ Gradually letting the muscles drop

√ Meditation

These methods can be used whenever you're worried because they don't require much time. Below are some anxiety and depression management activities for you to overcome your negative thinking.

4.2 Anxiety and Depression Management

Anxiety Worksheet

Write down situation, your actions and intensity of your anxiety.

Date: _____

What Happened

_____

_____

_____

How I Reacted

_____

_____

_____

How Bad is it Really?	What I Think/Feel	How I'd Like to React Next Time
Not Bad	_____	
	_____	_____
1	_____	_____
2	_____	_____
3	_____	_____
4	_____	_____
5	_____	_____
Really Bad	_____	_____

My Anxiety Levels

Use this worksheet to explore what happens to your body, thoughts, and feelings as your anxiety increases! Write down the helpful coping skills that you use for each level of anxiety.

Level 1   What happens when you first start feeling anxious?

Level 2   What happens as you become more anxious?

Level 3   What happens when you are at your most anxious?

How do you cope?

How to Cope with Anxiety?

Anxiety is a feeling of worry, nervousness, or unease about something with an uncertian outcome.

Answer the questions according to your own experience.

What has been the moment of your life in which you have felt the most anxiety?

What strategies do you use to cope with anxiety?

Do you think exams cause high level of anxiety? Why?

Do you remember the first time you felt axiety at school? How was it?

Imagine that you have a student who suffers from anxiety attacks before taking an exam. How would you help him cope?

Instead Of

What are some things that you can do differently this week when you are feeling anxious? Use this worksheet to come up with healthy coping skills to use for your anxiety triggers instead of responding the way that you usualy do.

This week, when I feel anxious. instead of...

(How do you usually cope with your anxiety?)

I will use these coping skills!

(Place a check mark next to each coping skill you use during the week)

☐ _____

☐ _____

☐ _____

☐ _____

☐ _____

I Can Cope With Feeling ANXIOUS

	Some thinngs that make me feel anxious are...
	1. _____
	2. _____
	3. _____

These changes happen when I feel anxious:

Changes in my body...	Thoughts I have...	Things I do...

When I feel anxious, I can cope by:

Check all of the coping skills that might be helpful! Use the blank spaces to write in your own.

☐ Deep breathing   ☐ Going for a walk   _____

☐ Using positive self-talk ☐ Writing in my journal   _____

☐ Meditating or relaxing   ☐ Practicing mindfulness   _____

☐ Talking to a friend   ☐ Thinking happy thoughts   _____

☐ Talking to an adult   ☐ Keeping myself busy   _____

☐ Playing a game   ☐ Exercising   _____

Anxiety Buster Worksheet

TOP STRESSES	WHAT CAN BE DONE?
Pay attention to "what ifs," Ask yourself "what is" instead of worrying about imagined senarios. If there's nothing to be done, worrying won't help.	
------------------------------	------------------------------
------------------------------	------------------------------
------------------------------	------------------------------

TO DO: Write everything swirling in your mind. Seeing it on paper helps things seem more manageable.

------------------------------	------------------------------
------------------------------	------------------------------
------------------------------	------------------------------

TOP 3 PRIORITIES TODAY: Instead of trying to do it all, pick. Accomplishment increases dopamine!

☐ 1. _____   ☐ 2. _____   ☐ 3. _____

GRATEFUL FOR	PRAYING FOR
When we feel grateful, our brain releases oxytocin. There is space to write names of those things you thought that you would pray for and forgot or those subjects dear to your heart. Too much self focus is not helpful.	
------------------------------	------------------------------
------------------------------	------------------------------
------------------------------	------------------------------

FIGHT FEAR ☐ Pray ☐ Go outside ☐ Take intentional deep breaths ☐ Exercise ☐ Turn off screens ☐ Eat a healthy diet ☐ Visit a friend ☐ Act of kindness

CHAPTER 5 GET STRESS RELIEF WITH COGNITIVE THERAPY

When faced with problems in life, we all experience some level of stress naturally. We can navigate stress-inducing circumstances without too much discomfort when we feel confident and in control.

However, stress levels can increase in many circumstances, such as while under long-term stress or after a catastrophic event. This is because stress has multiple adverse consequences on both mental and physical health. Stress symptoms can start to have an impact on overall health which makes it challenging to deal with specific or routine life situations, such as overwhelming anxiety, racing heartbeat, and uneasy stomach, etc.

Cognitive Therapy (CBT) is a form of talk therapy that aims to improve one's mental and emotional health by changing one's perspective on their own condition. This fresh perspective can help one to regain a sense of self-contentment, mitigate distressing symptoms, and learn effective methods of handling stressful situations with composure and assurance. This chapter will cover the stress management activities for kids to deal with their stress levels.

5.1 Stress Management and CBT
Stress Management

WHAT IS STRESS?

Stress happens when you have strong feelings of being worried, anxious, or overwhelmed!

Stress buttons or triggers are things that happen that cause you to feel stresses out.

WHAT ARE YOUR TOP FIVE STRESS BUTTONS?

1. _____

2. _____

3. _____

4. _____

5. _____

WHERE DO YOU FEEL STRESS IN YOUR BODY?

WHERE IS YOUR RELAXING PLACE?

STRESS HAPPENS WHEN YOU HAVE:

STRESS HAPPENS WHEN YOU HAVE:

- a lot of things going on at once

- an important decision to make

- an unexpected change in your life

- a big event coming up

- something really dangerous or terrifying happen to you

GOOD WAYS TO COPE WITH STRESS!

Figure out your stress button.

Take a time-out from whatever is stressing you out.

Talk to an adult.

Practice relaxation to help your body calm down.

Listen to music or watch a movie.

Keep a Stress Journal.

Use positive self-talk!

_____

Frustrated

Feeling Frustrated Means:

Very angry, discouraged, or upset because of being unable to do or complete somrthing

WHEN I AM FEELING FRUSTRATED:

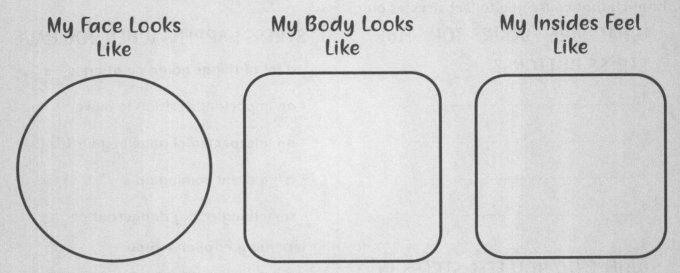

My Face Looks Like

My Body Looks Like

My Insides Feel Like

WHAT MAKES ME FEEL FRUSTRATED:

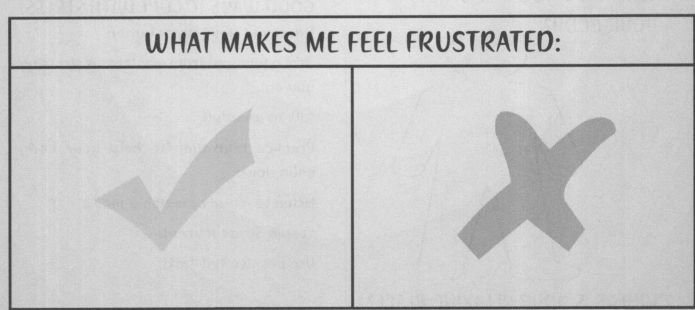

That Really Stressed Me Out

Situation	I experienced this within the last year	Good Stress (situation motivated you to prepared and do your best)	Bad Stress (situation made you feel overwhelmed and worried most of the time).
Meeting new people			
Being peer pressured			
Fighting with friends or siblings			
Failing a test			
Fighting with friends or siblings			
Failing a test			
Giving a presentation			
Engaged in several activities			
Parents arguing			
Feeling left out			
Moving			
Being teased			

Read through the situations below and each one that you experienced within last year.Mark whether the situation led to good stress or bad stress.

If you checked the 'bad stress' box more than three times, you might be experiencing stress overload. Talk to trusted adult.

Calm Down Bottle

Name : _____   Date : _____

Instructions: Fill one third of a small plastic bottle with warm water. Add 2 ounces glitter glue, 2-4 ounces fine glitter, and 2-3 drops food coloring. Close the lid tightly and shake to combine. When you're upset, look at the bottle and breathe deeply.

After making a calm down bottle, answer the following questions:

1. What is a calm down bottle?

2. How will you use your calm down bottle?

3. When will you use your calm down bottle?

4. Draw a picture of your calm down bottle:

Improving Behavior

Behaviour I Need to Work on at Home

Why I Need to Work on this Behaviour

2 Things I can do to Improve This Behaviour

Take Control

Write down methods to manage your frustration and to stay calm.

How I Manage Frustration

How I Stay Calm

How I Manage Frustration

5.2 Mindfulness and CBT

One of the most frequent problems that kids and teens bring up in treatment is anxiety, which can co-occur with other problems or disorders. The relaxation techniques listed below can aid your child in overcoming stress or anxiety.

1. Practice Deep Breathing

Numerous easy deep breathing exercises are available that may be done at home. To practice deep breathing at home:

√ Take a five-second deep breath through your nose.

√ Take a deep breath and hold it for five seconds.

√ Take a 5-second mouth-to-mouth exhalation.

√ Repeat.

This technique, which you can use to calm your breathing and lower your pulse rate when you're feeling anxious in social situations without calling attention to yourself, can be used for 5 to 10 minutes at a time.

2. Grounding

This imagery-guided grounding practice can be used to reduce anxiety as well as to keep the focus on the present moment by looking for sensory stimulation in your immediate surroundings:

Consider a location that gives you comfort to start. A beloved area, a beach, or a childhood memory could be found somewhere in your home. Spend the next 5–10 minutes picturing the location you have imagined.

Ask yourself the following questions while using your five senses.

√ Do you see anything? Take a moment to scan your surroundings and this area. What is it you can make out in the distance? What can you see right beside you? Try to pay attention to little things you might ordinarily overlook.

√ Do you hear anything? Take careful note of the sounds you hear. Do you hear quiet or loud noises? Are they audible nearby or far away?

√ How about your palate? Do you consume food or liquids? What does it taste like, if so? Is it savory or sweet?

√ How are you feeling? Is it hot or cold? Does there exist a breeze? Is the sun warming your skin as it shines on you? Or do you have a cozy blanket covering you? Pay attention to the sensations around you.

√ What scent do you detect? What scent is in the air here? Is the aroma powerful or subtle? You should pay attention to and enjoy the scents you notice.

These practices help you unwind. In times of tension or anxiety, spend as much time as necessary picturing your cozy space. Let yourself experience security and peace.

3. Progressive Muscle Relaxation

The gradual muscle relaxation technique is a simple one to practice at home:

Feet: firmly curl your toes, hold for five seconds, and then let go. The feet should be pointed, held for five seconds, and then released.

Thighs: Tightly contract your thighs, hold the contraction for five seconds, and then release.

Torso: Contract your abdominal muscles, hold for 5 seconds, and then relax.

Back: Squeeze together your shoulder blades for five seconds, then release.

Shoulders: Squeeze your shoulders together as you lift them toward your ears, hold for five seconds, and then release.

Arms: Squeeze the muscles in your arms by making fists and bending your arms so that your forearm is next to your biceps. Hold for five seconds, then release.

Hands: Curl your fingers into your palms to form a tight fist. Hold for five seconds, then release.

Face: Twist and draw your facial features toward the center of your face. Hold for five seconds, then let go.

Full body: Squeeze and tighten every muscle in your body at once, hold for five seconds, then release.

CHAPTER 6 PARENTS' GUIDE TO TACKLE ANXIETY AND STRESS

When children have worried thoughts, grownups in their lives frequently intervene to remedy the problem.

Isn't it sensible to keep kids away from the Pitbull next door if they're afraid of dogs?

No, not at all.

You're supporting and fueling their worry by assisting them in avoiding scary situations. They're also missing out on chances to practice coping techniques and prove that they can handle the worrying thought or feeling the next time it arises. Helping your child learn to manage anxiety is the finest thing you can do for them.

How you react to your child's worry will significantly impact how they develop to cope with anxiety.

6.1 Validate Their Feelings

That's easy to say things like, "Oh, it's not a big issue," or "Don't stress about it," when your child expresses concern about something. "You're going to be OK." Such reactions provide the message that your child's emotions are incorrect.

Instead, confirm their feelings by saying something like, "It seems like you are nervous right now," or "I'd be anxious too if I had to speak in front of a large crowd."

Then, despite their anxiousness, write a message expressing your confidence in their ability to achieve. "It's difficult to undertake scary things like this," and then add, "but I am sure you can do it."

6.2 Tackle Negative Thoughts

Your child, like adults, is vulnerable to negative thinking. This negative thinking can make them anxious and lower their self-esteem.

You may educate them on identifying bad emotions, challenging them, and using positive self-talk to convert them into happy, realistic ones.

√ Embrace it. They must first be able to recognize a negative idea before they may address it. Assist them in making a shortlist of unpleasant thoughts that they frequently have.

√ Put it to the test. Encourage your youngster to think of themselves as a detective, gathering evidence to evaluate the evidence behind their worrisome thoughts. For instance, if they often tell themselves, "Is it true that I'm stupid?" they should ask themselves. Am I an idiot? Have there been moments when I've demonstrated my intelligence?" It will teach them not to believe every bad thought that enters their minds.

√ It should be corrected. The final phase is to replace their negative self-talk with a positive one after recognizing and challenging it. "Oh dear, you're not stupid," don't say straight away. They will not only refuse to trust you, but they will also refuse to learn how to change their anxious thoughts. "What would you say to a colleague who believed they were stupid?" instead. Urge them to tell themselves the same thing when they respond with kindness.

6.3 Real Threats and False Alarms

Discuss with your kid how anxiety serves to keep them safe. For example, if a tiger were hunting them, their brain would send a warning signal to their body. They might experience physical changes like sweaty palms and a faster heart rate. As they were ready to run from the tiger, they would feel a surge of energy (a real threat).

Then inform them that their brain can also set up a false warning at times. They may experience great panic due to these false alarms, even if the scenario isn't life-or-death. Examples of false alarms include trying out for a basketball game, speaking in front of a large group, or preparing for a huge test. Explain that if there is a serious threat, they should pay attention to the warning signs and take steps to protect themselves. If it's a false alarm, confronting their anxieties is good.

6.4 The Stepladder Approach

Anxious children will frequently go to great efforts to avoid their anxieties. Unfortunately, avoiding them simply makes them more anxious. Although it may be frightening at first, confronting anxieties will help you overcome anxiety in the long term.

If your child is scared of something specific, such as sleeping alone in the dark or making new friends, use the stepladder approach to help them face their anxieties with one small step at a time. The idea of this strategy is for them to perform something reasonably scary—and then practice it until it becomes less scary. They can then proceed to the next level.

Make a list with your child of the actions they can take to tackle their fears and achieve their overall objective. If your child has been sleeping in your bed, here's an idea of how you might assist them in overcoming their fear of sleeping alone:

1. Place a mattress on the floor next to your bed for your child to sleep on.

2. Let your child sleep on the floor, but put it closer to the middle and away from the bed.

3. Allow your child to sleep on a mat on the floor in the room, knowing that you will place them in their bed after falling asleep.

4. Allow your child to fall asleep in their room with you present.

5. Allow your child to fall asleep in their room with the understanding that you will monitor them every few minutes until they fall asleep.

6. Allow your youngster to fall asleep with the light on in their room.

7. Allow your youngster to sleep with only a nightlight in their room.

You might give your child a special privilege or incentive if they reach a certain milestone. Natural repercussions can also be used to motivate your youngster. For instance, if they are hesitant to order ice cream, you could tell them they must do it if they want it. Of course, you should only use this if you're confident in their ability to accomplish it independently.

6.5 Change the Channel

If your child is worrying about something they can't control, such as the possibility that it will rain tomorrow, causing a football match to be canceled, let them distract themselves.

"*Is there something you can do about that?*" ask your youngster when they are focused on a specific concern. If the answer is affirmative, assist them in resolving the issue.

For instance, studying might be excellent if they're afraid of a science test. They could also practice their talents if they're afraid about not making the basketball squad.

If they're concerned about things they can't control, such as the weather or another person's actions, remind them that the only thing they can handle is how they react. Discuss how they might deal with poor weather or how they could react if someone is cruel to them.

Then, assist them in diverting their attention away from the subject. Help them change channels to change the mood. Constant worrying will leave them caught in a state of tension.

6.6 Be Aware of Your Parenting Style

Because some parenting styles can exacerbate your child's anxiety, it's critical to examine your parenting style and relationships with your child. Both authoritarian and liberal parenting styles are associated with an increased incidence of depression and anxiety in children.

Expecting perfection and having complete control over your child's actions is a definite way to cause worry in both yourself and your child. It can make your child feel pressured to succeed all the time, leaving them immobilized with anxiety and self-doubt.

Boundary-free parenting, on the other hand, is rarely the solution. Permissive parenting devolves so much power to the child's decisions that it might cause uneasiness. Allowing your child to deal with life's everyday problems helps them build more resiliency and appropriate coping mechanisms.

CONCLUSION

Mental disorders in children are prevalent. Some of the exhibits of these conditions include PTSD, chronic anxiety, generalized anxiety disorder, and particular phobias. Around 4 million children aged three to seventeen years in the United States (almost 7 percent of the population) suffer from anxiety.

Mental disorders are relatively treatable, but they go undetected and unrecognized far too often. Consult your doctor if you suspect your child has an anxiety issue. Your child's physician may send them to a mental health specialist for help.

Each Mental disorder has its list of symptoms and, as a result, treatment. Anxiety is usually treated with cognitive therapy but can also be treated with medication. A mental health expert can assist your child in developing skills to cope with anxious feelings and gaining confidence in confronting some of his anxieties.

Consult a specialist if your child's anxiousness lasts longer than two weeks. You should consult a psychiatrist if your child's anxiety is hurting with daily functioning.

For example, if their anxiety affects their school attendance or grades or they cannot participate in social activities due to their concerns, they may require professional assistance.

A therapist will almost certainly want you to participate in treatment so that you may learn how to help your kid at home. You may learn particular ways to coach your child when they're worried, or you could learn how to help them healthily face their anxieties.

While dealing with your child's Mental health issues can be difficult and exhausting for many parents, the best part is that they can conquer it with this anxiety workbook. Following these strategies and providing connection and support to your child can go a long way toward empowering them. They will learn that their parents will listen to their problems and provide them with validation, tools, and assistance. Help your kids with the activities, exercises, and worksheets to deal with their mental health issues.

THANK YOU

Made in the USA
Coppell, TX
06 June 2023

17772029R00044